Polymer Clay for Beginners

A Step by Step Guide to Craft 20 Polymer Clay
Projects with Tools and Techniques to Get You
Started

By

Laurel Fennimore

Disclaimer

This publication is designed to provide competent and reliable information regarding the subject matter covered. However, the views expressed in this publication are those of the author alone, and should not be taken as expert instruction or professional advice. The reader is responsible for his or her own actions.

The author hereby disclaims any responsibility or liability whatsoever that is incurred from the use or application of the contents of this publication by the purchaser or reader. The purchaser or reader is hereby responsible for his or her own actions.

Table of Contents

Introduction

If you are new to polymer clay, be ready for a really good treat. This is one art of endless possibilities. It exposes you comprehensively to a world of limitless artistic inventions, innovations, and experiments. There is no boundary to your creativity and ingenuity. This clay is used to do so many things than you know. With this clay, you can model, and mold all manner of complex products.

No doubt, we are highly indebted to early polymer clay inventors. I mean, if not for them, we won't have been introduced to this beautiful art treasure.

This is not children's putty as it seems, it is a classic art used in sculpturing artworks. For many years, clay has been a craft material commonly used by children to play. It is amazing that this play craft can also be used to make useful and interesting projects used in decoration and for ornaments. Children majorly use this clay in experimenting with different forms of mold and shapes that can be made. It lets them birth their imagination to reality, if not perfectly, at least it allows them to try.

Polymer clay includes little clay minerals like mineral clay liquid. This man-made clay can be used anywhere and at any time. This clay is mixed with a plasticizer for flexibility, and various kinds of fillers for texture and color. Due to its pliability, it can be used to mold different shapes of jewelry, and sculpture. This clay is nontoxic, and can be molded in the home.

There are very few tools used in working with polymer clays. You don't need to go spending all your earnings to acquire molding tools, some of the tools you need are right in your home. After baking, the polymer clay can be enhanced in appearance through sanding, painting, buffing or glazing.

Your only limitation in polymer crafts is your imagination. There are a thousand project ideas you can try. Each one is more uniquely different from the other.

Also, it will interest you to know that polymer clay is so cheap. You can make amazing jewelry with just a little money. Making your own jewelry with polymer clay is way cheaper than buying an already made bead or jewelry. Yeah, you can read that again.

Tell me why you won't be delighted to make your own jewelry yourself at a very affordable amount.

Expect to have some crazy fun using this amazing craft material.

Chapter 1

What is Polymer Clay?

Polymer clay is a man-made clay that consists of polyvinyl chloride (PVC) base. In other words, it is an artificial plastic polymer. PVC is one of the most popular and widely used plastic.

PVC is used to make many things around us today, they make up most of your children's toys, and plastic water pipes.

Asides from the plastic component in polymer, the other components of polymer clay are coloring, filers, and resins. They are responsible for their soft texture, unique color and great flexibility.

When freshly manufactured, it is a wet-dry malleable lump, and unlike the natural clay, you don't need to mix it with water. However, it tends to get dry and hard if it stays for a long time.

All polymer is free of nuts, latex, wheat, dairy, gluten, and sulfur. It is ingestible. There are different brands of polymer clay, and all of them comes with manufacturer's specification for use. As a molder, you have to be careful to follow the specification of the brand of the product you are using.

This clay is more sturdy and versatile than natural clay. You can use it in molding more things and household materials than natural clay can ever produce. Also, it is easier to use, you don't have to fire polymer clay in a kiln to give it shape. It has great stamina on its own, irrespective of the type of polymer clay it is. All you need to cure your mold is a little heat, which you can get from a toaster oven or even your local oven used at home. It can bake as little as 275* F.

Also when exposed to room temperature or a cold atmosphere, it doesn't bake itself or becomes hardened. You could definitely leave it out and get back to it the same way you left it. You just have to beware of any condition above room temperature.

It will amaze you that the artificial clay that started with polymer clay is now lost in the records of countless research chemists who made their own experiments with synthetic plastic compounds. However, there are other types of clay that are usually mistaken with polymer clay.

One of which is the modeling clay. The modeling clay is an oil-based compound while the polymer clay is a polyvinyl chloride plastic-based material. They are both similar in a way, as they are both available in a variety of colors. However, polymer clay has a more unique, and a larger variety of colors.

The modeling clay can be used time after time, it doesn't dry out after modeling. This is unlike the polymer clay that thickens and hardens when it is baked. Even before it is baked, if left open, and exposed to harsh temperature, it could dry quickly and become tough to use. You would need to use additives to soften the clay again. The modeling clay as a stark opposite is very malleable even after molding. Modeling clay is a great material for beginners in molding craft to use. It allows you to make a couple of mistakes with one clay mixture, as you can always re-use the clay, even after curing. It is majorly used in making temporary products.

Polymer clay is a fun and popularly used craft material for sharpening one's creative ability. This material is so versatile that you can build almost anything with it, this is no exaggeration. You could use this craft material for several years and still feel like you are only tapping the surface, because the more you practice, the more you realize that there are indeed no limits to what you can create using this material.

It can be used for creativity hunts by special artists, and craftsmen. It is also a fun tool for children to feel their imaginary words.

History of Polymer Clay

Polymer clay has been around for over forty years now; it was invented sometime around 1930. Though, there were many individual experiments by different people that led to the global recognition and existence of polymer clay.

All form of moldings before this time was done with natural clay, artificial clay was still a new thing. Some of the polymer clays started as inventions from local artists. These inventions were made through experiments.

One successful experiment was done by a doll maker in Germany who was the daughter of a famous doll maker at the time, named Fifi Rehbinder.

It happened that there was a war uproar in the city then, so her regular doll making supplies were disrupted due to the political upheavals in the country. So couldn't get access to her supplies, and was quite stranded in her production process, so she began to experiment with alternatives to some of her supplies so that she could go on with production. As the very resourceful woman that she was, she started experimenting with plastic clay. The experiment turned out to be successful, and she called the plastic clay Fifi Mosaik. She began using it in sculpting doll heads and other parts of the doll. This was just the beginning of the invention of the polymer.

In 1964, she sold the formula she normally used in her production of plastic clay to another artist named Eberhard Faber. He went on to tweak the formula and produce a different brand of polymer clay. It was generally accepted as the main tool used in making dolls.

A similar experiment was conducted in the United States. Ellen Rixford tells in her book how a clay illustrator experimented with vinyl dough. They were the first readily available polymer clay products in the USA using polyform products. These were originally formulated for potential; use to conduct heat far away from the cores of electric transformers in electrical appliances. They were made to be thermal transfer compound.

In 1975, a family in the united states received Fimo all the way from Germany as a Christmas gift. They started using it in making dolls and other crafts. In no time, it started to become popular.

This experiment was carried out in the early 1960s by a few clay illustrators, and unfortunately, it wasn't successful for this particular intention. The whole compound was later shelved away, although it was just for the brief moment. It was totally forgotten about until a little girl who happened to be the daughter of the owner of the compound, that formerly tried using it as an electrical conductor, picked it. She found it in her father's office, one day when she came visiting and used it to play dirty.

It was after she was caught, that it was discovered that the polyform, also known as Sculpey could be used as a modeling or molding compound.

Today, several types of polymer clay have been formed for molding craft, different art pieces, and sculptures.

How Does Polymer Clay Work?

Polymer clay is used in making household and commercial art materials. There are different techniques for making different things with polymer clay.

However, every process begins with conditioning or mixing the clay with chemicals and other additives. The clay is massaged and conditioned in such a way that it retains its thickness or flexibility texture. During conditioning, it must be massaged gently and carefully. Afterward, it is detailed with sculpting tools, and molded into the desired shape. After it is shaped, it is perfected with basic cutting tools.

Once the clay has taken shape, it is placed into the oven to be cured or baked. The oven should be set at the required temperature, and consistently monitored until the clay is well cured.

The clay mold needs over 15 minutes to cure properly.

Your polymer craft is ready. This is how polymer works.

Application Areas of Polymer Clay

The possibility available to the usefulness of polymer clay is limitless. It is much easier to work with for making basic, and essential products like jewelry, and an assortment of crafts like home decoration tools, pottery, scrapbooking, and sculpture.

- It is basically used to make beads, holiday ornaments, keychains, figurines, doll jewelry, miniatures, wall art, garden décor, candle holders, keepsake boxes, journal covers, bookmarks, cloth embellishments and other creative shapes.
- You can also make a professional career in polymer clay. Many polymer artists today are living fine and financially independent. Art is in itself a lucrative field that you can monetize.
- Polymer clay allows for creativity, it allows you to create your own design in decoration.
- It can be used as a material for hands-on activity by children.
- Polymer clay also makes a perfect substitute for glass in jewelry making. You can simply make this in the comfort of your house, without having to look for open flame, and you would still get a very gorgeous result if you massage it well.

- You can mold it into the shape of gemstones, glass, and marble using a variety of unique techniques, and a mixture of clay. Also, it assures more durability than other production materials like glass.
- It is used to make highly versatile products like toys, baby dolls, art sculptures, and jewelry.
- You can also use it to design an already made project with the clay, and make a decorative inscription.
- Also, you can use this in decorating the picture frame with polymer clay letters or your pen to make homework sessions fun.

Polymer clay is largely versatile and can be used for many things. If you can think of it, you can do it.

Chapter 2

Terms Used in Polymer Clay

Just like in every craft, there are basic terms you are bound to come in contact with time after time, as you practice and learn your craft.

Some of these terms are familiar, and you must have encountered them on a daily basis, or possibly used them, while others will totally seem strange and foreign to you. We will be explaining all of these terms and what they imply in polymer craft.

- Translucent or Trans

    Polymer clay comes in many types of colors; some interestingly dark and some with a very dark or dense appearance. Some of these colors include pearlescent and metallic varieties. Most brands of polymer clay include a colorless translucent variety. This variety is very unique in itself, and amazingly so. When light shines through the translucent clay after baking, it has an appearance like that of frosted milk glass. Although no brand of polymer clay is transparent like glass, some brands give this translucent color that makes it seem like they are transparent when they are not.

- TLS (Translucent Liquid Sculpey)

The is one of the first brands of liquid clay (and the only one for many years) was Translucent Liquid Sculpey. It is still very much available today, though the name has changed in some locations.

- Plasticizer

This is one essential component of polymer clay. As a plastic chemical, polymer contains a plasticizer to make it flexible. It is a liquid substance that allows the clay to be malleable and pliable. This plasticizer makes the plastic to be strong after baking, rather than rough and brittle. Hence, the plasticizer is what prevents the clay from cracking and shattering after it has been baked.

- Condition

Polymer clay comes in a stiff gelled up form and is bound to crumble if you work with it in that form. Hence, the process of making your clay workable and pliable for use is called conditioning. There are different means of conditioning polymer clay. You can use your hands or an acrylic roller. Another professional machine you can use is the pasta machine. These machines will help to condition your clay well till it is soft and pliable, ready to be worked into a beautiful polymer craft.

- Pasta Machine

The pasta machine is a great gift that you can give to yourself or every lover of polymer clay art. It is also used to sheet noodles and linguine. It is made in Italy and yeah it is quite affordable too.

- Acrylic Rod

This is a special type of rolling pin used for polymer clay. It is special because unlike other conventional wooden rolling pins, it doesn't absorb the clay oils, neither does it react with the clay. It is a great tool used in flattening polymer clay.

- Leaching

If you are working with a factory fresh polymer clay, it is bound to be too soft as a result of the lucidity of the clay oil. Hence, you have to remove the excess of these oils and plasticizer by leaching. Leaching is done by laying the clay between two plain sheets of paper and placing a heavy object on top of it to forcefully exert the oil.

- Clay Softener

Clay Softeners are bottles of plasticizer and liquid chemicals that are used in making hard blocks of polymer clay pliable and more workable. It was initially called Clay Diluent. The term is still being used today.

- Mud Clay

This is not a natural earthen clay as it seems. Mud clay is a term used in describing a blah-colored clay that you get when you mix clay scraps. Depending on the colors used in your project, mud clay is usually dull pinky brown.

Mud is generally a polymer clay term used in describing dull clay you get after mixing all your scraps together.

- Extruder

This tool is used in shaping polymer clay. You can use it to squirt polymer clay in a round, square, snake shape, or any other complex shapes. There are different types of extruders used in making specific shapes. Extruder is also used to carry out different polymer techniques.

- Mica Shift

This is a technique used in creating an optical illusion where a smooth surface looks like it has raised designs. It is mostly used in metallic polymer clay.

- Mokume Gane

  This is another polymer clay technique used in making special types of polymer clay patterned designs. To make this, layers or sheets of polymer clay are stacked, and compressed into a stack or block. In the end, it reveals complex wavy patterns, and these slices are used to make patterned designs in your projects.

- Skinner blend

  This technique is named after Judith Skinner who invented it. This is a blended color sheet of polymer clay that graduates from one color to another. There are different ways of making Skinner blends

- Cane

  In glassworking, these canes are also called murrine. This is a log of polymer clay that has an image or design running the entire length. It has similar to slice-and-bake cookies. On all slices of a cane will reveal the same image. When you reduce a cane, the log becomes smaller, and the slices become a smaller version of the image.

- Millefiori

This is an Italian term for thousand flowers, it is used in glasswork and polymer clay to arrange slices of canes to create a pretty design. It is what you make cane from cane slices. You make the Millefiori effect from polymer clay canes.

- Texture Sheet

Texture sheet is a term used in describing different types of unmounted stamp, it is pressed into the polymer clay to give it a texture. Texture sheets are also called texture mats, and they can be processed with the pasta machine along with clay, to get a deep impression.

- Tissue Blade

This is a super sharp blade used in making designed cuts in techniques like slicing canes or making mica shift or mokume-gane. This blade was by artists borrowed from the medical field. They are very sharp blades used in slicing tissue in histology for microscopic imaging. They get dull. For this reason, you have to save tissue blades for these specialty purposes.

- Sutton Slice

This technique was developed by Lisa Pavelka, and it involves molding a texture sheet and pressing clay into the design. The clay is then removed and pressed onto another sheet, giving a raised pattern.

- Veneer

In woodworking, this is the layering of attractive and expensive wood over cheaper wood to keep the costs down. The same idea is replicated in polymer craft, it involves the layering of a pretty sheet of clay over scrap clay. These pretty sheets of clay are called veneers. They are decorative clay sheets that can be used in making shapes, pendants, earrings and other decorative pieces. They are usually stored to be used in the future.

- Baking/Curing

These two terms mean the same thing and are interchangeably used. Different people call it baking, others call it curing. Whichever it is, this process refers to the heating of polymer clay into the oven. Some persons are offended about the term because it sounds amateurish to the ears. Curing is the most popular word used in describing the process of hardening the clay and making it solid. The word baking came around from the baking process, anything that is processed in an oven is said to be baked. Anything processed with heat is said to be baked.

- Tenting

This term is used in describing the act of covering your item during baking. It is usually done in some special techniques to reduce the effect of the heat on the clay. This name comes from the practice of using a makeshift material like cardboard or foil to create a tent over the clay. It simply involves covering your clay with items during baking.

- Quenching

This technique is believed to make translucent clay more clear. It involved plunging hot clay straight from the oven into ice water. Though some other people believe it makes clay stronger, it actually doesn't.

- Heat gun

Heat gun is very similar to a blow dryer, but it has much more heat and less fan power. It is used in different ways when working with polymer clay. Some of these ways are popping resin bubbles, melting embossing powder, drying alcohol ink, and clearing liquid polymer clay finishes. Although an embossing heat tool can do almost this exact work for some processes, you might prefer the heat gun that comes in variable heat and variable speed model.

- Ramp Baking

  This technique is not so popular as it is totally unnecessary. However, it is a good try to solve frustrating browning or cracking issues. Ramp baking refers to the act of placing an item into a cold oven and gradually increasing the temperature over a long period of time.

- Plaques

  This term is used to describe moon-shaped bubbles that appear in baked translucent polymer clay. These bubbles are a result of the gases that are collected within the clay mass during baking. It happens with all types of clay molds but it is most commonly seen in translucent clay. It is also called moonies.

- Armature

Sometimes, clay is built over makeshift skeletons to give it a lightweight heavy look. These skeletons are called armature. It is a support that a sculpture is built over. It can be made from wire, aluminum foil, or cardboard. Armatures are not used to prevent breakage, but rather to help the clay take due shape and gain support. An example of a popular armature is the fool core made from aluminum.

- Highlighting

This is an interesting process in polymer where you apply a light or metallic paint as a finishing element in your claying. It makes your clay look dynamic and amazing.

- Gilding Cream or Paste

This cream is used as a highlight wax on textured areas of an item.

They are different types of gilding pastes m used in giving highlights to texture.

- Resin

  Resin is a very broad name for all the components used in making up many plastics. It is also used to refer to any type of material that hardens to a glossy surface.

- Glaze, sealer, varnish

  These three terms refer to tools used in giving polymer clay a shiny and glossy finish. It is also used to give the clay a protective body from water and oil. Although, polymer clay does not need to be sealed, neither does it need a glaze. It is naturally shiny and has a clean protective look. It can't get destroyed by water, but using a varnish or glaze just gives it that extra good and shiny appearance. You just have to be careful to select the ones that align with your clay. Some kind of glaze could make your clay sticky and destroy its shiny appearance.

- Silkscreen

The silkscreen is a stencil that's attached to fine mesh fabric. This is a technique where a silkscreen is pressed to the surface of polymer clay and bright color of paint is pressed through it, such that the design of the silkscreen is seen on the polymer clay.

Chapter 3

Tips and Tricks in Polymer Clay Crafts

Polymer clay is pretty fun but could be quite tasking and technical as you go higher. There are many technical projects as much as there are simple projects. As a beginner, you won't want to come up front against the magnitudes of projects unprepared. Listed here is a long number of tips and tricks that you can try out to help you make complex projects easily.

You can also apply some of these tips in your basic project, they are just existent to help you make amazing projects easily.

Be careful to go through all of them carefully, and you can just get a lump of clay to practice and ascertain the effectiveness of these tips and increase your professionalism.

Polymer clay is an extremely versatile medium, which is perfect for beginners and professional artists alike. It can be a challenging and complex medium for those who want to push the limits. But it is also very easy for beginners and newbies to get good results, once you know a few tips and tricks. Here are some helpful polymer clay tips for beginners.

1. Smoothing the surface of your clay

Sometimes, the surface of your clay project might become rough after molding, there might be fingerprints stain, unintended impressions, slight aberrations, and other forms of indentions. These indentions could affect the appearance of your mold and make it appear rougher than it actually is. To correct this and make the surface areas of your clay smooth, you will need some alcohol. Yes, it is proven that alcohol melts polymer clay. However, you won't want to melt away all the upper part of the clay. That will be a larger mess than the already existing problem you are trying to solve. To dilute the effect of the alcohol on your clay, put your paintbrush into a small plate of alcohol mixed with water. You will need to add a little water to the alcohol to diffuse its harshness. Then, dip your paintbrush into the mixture.

Move the paintbrush around the surface of the clay and watch it diffuse easily. Be careful to apply it only where you need it. Rubbing the paintbrush on already smooth areas in the clay can deform the shape of the clay and lessen the size.

Note: This can only be successful before the clay is baked. After it has been baked, it is impossible to smoothen the surface of your clay using this method.

2. Keep your sculpture workable

Unlike the normal earthen clay, polymer doesn't dry out quickly. However, the warmth of your hands while can soften it so much that it threatens to become sticky and melt. What do you do? Pause your sculpting and put your sculpture in the fridge for about 10 minutes. This will get it ready to be sculpted again.

3. Softening clay

Sometimes your clay could come in a hard rocky form that is impossible to use. For you to use a pack of clay in molding it has to be softened enough to be pliable. The more pliable your clay is, the higher its usability or productivity. You can only use the clay when it is softened. This is why you should ensure you go for soft clays only. But what happens when the clay you got happened to be hardened, like rock hard? Do you discard it? well, I don't think you should when there is a means to soften the texture and make it more pliable. To quickly and easily soften your clay, place it in a resealable plastic bag and place it inside your bag for 30 minutes. Then run the resalable bag under hot water for 2-3 minutes. You have your soft clay ready. However, be careful not to do it so much that your clay turns liquid.

4. Hand Sanitizer cleans clay residue off your hands

Molding with polymer clay could lead to several implications like having the residue of clay on your hands after molding. Sometimes, this residue proves adamant to soap and water and would need a harder solution to get all of it off totally.

Now, tip one would be relevant in this case. Remember we said that alcohol dissolves polymer clay. Hence, some alcohol-based sanitizer will do the magic beyond your expectations.

Press some alcohol-based hand sanitizer gel into your hands, leave for a few minutes, and wipe them off with a paper towel. Afterward, use a soap and water wash and all the residues are gone like they were never there.

5. The cornstarch.

This is one golden tip, that remains priceless at all times. The cornstarch has several uses and is a great aid to the artist. It is very useful in smoothing the corners of your clay mold before baking. It makes a great mold release for all forms of molds and texture sheets. To smooth the sides of your mold, all you need is to apply a little cornstarch on your finger and gently move your hand around the clay, so that every part of the clay mold comes in contact with the cornstarch. This process will totally smooth every fingerprint off of your clay creations. Also, to prevent your beads from browning or scorching when baking, you can bury them in a bed of cornstarch as you bake.

6. Firming up your polymer clay.

We've already discussed how to soften your polymer clay. However, it is also possible that your polymer clay is too soft and mushy that it seems to be dripping or to be too light for the project you want to use it for. Before you rush to discard and go get a new one, let's try firming that mushy clay up. This process is called leaching. To leach clay, you place the clay between two plain papers and then put a book on top of it for a few hours to exert the excess oil or liquid chemicals from the clay so all the excess moisture you don't need is absorbed by the paper. Keep monitoring it until you have achieved the consistency that you want. The longer you let your leach be, the more moisture is removed from the clay and leached into the paper and out of the clay. This will cause your clay to firmer, as the moisture has been removed. Don't do it too much so your clay doesn't get rock hard and crumbly.

7. You really do need an oven thermometer.

I think I need to emphasize the need for an oven thermometer here. Yes, I know you might be able to read the temperature of your oven yourself and monitor it very closely. However, you really do need this tool for accuracy. They are actually indispensable if you would get your molding right. And one awesome thing is that it isn't that expensive. You can get them at a very cheap rate.

However, for whatsoever amount you get them, they are pricelessly indispensable, as they save you a lot of troubles. Baking clay at the wrong temperature could mar your whole project and make a mess of all your stress and energy. In clay, accuracy really counts. You have to bake the clay long enough for it to be solid and sturdy. If the temperature is too low for your project, it could make it spongy and brittle. On the other hand, clay is susceptible to burning, and a very high temperature might completely toast your polymer.

Hence, your oven thermometer is an invaluable resource you must add to your tool collections.

8. Store properly.

Polymer clay is very non-toxic and can dissolve some plastics. Hence, if you must store your polymer clay in a bag, store it in plain old Ziploc sandwich bags. They are polymer clay safe and allows you to zip the bag shut, and prevent dust from affecting the clay.

Can you use plastic storage containers that aren't airtight? Yup but there's one caveat – they need to be slightly translucent (not totally clear) and have the recycling numbers of 2, 4, or 5 on the bottom.

So yes, plastic baggies are a great solution to storing your clay. Just keep them out of direct light and away from heat and you'll be fine.

Do not store in cardboard sheets.

9. Use white scrap clay to clean your hands and pasta machine.

Clay is a thick substance that can get dirty because of the moisture contained in it. Hence, when working with bright colored white polymer, you won't want to have dirt stains on it as it reduces the quality of your mold.

Your clay can be contaminated with fibers, dirt, or residue from other clay colors you molded that are glued to your hands or pasta machine. Here's an easy solution for you to solve. To prevent stains on your clay while working, take a ball of white scrap clay. It doesn't have to be large, just something tiny and significant. Massage and roll it in between your hands. This white ball will pick up every contaminant from your palm. Run the white ball through your pasta machine also, so that it can pick up any leftover colors, dirt, dust and fibers there. You can use this scrap clay consistently for the same purpose but you have to store it properly. You can store it in a Ziploc bag.

10. Crumpled aluminum foil makes a good bead core.

Large beads and figurines can require really large cores. You can have your mass of clay and use aluminum foil as a bead or figurine core. All you need to do is to crumple the foil tightly, then wrap the clay around the foil. Wrap it carefully in a way that all parts of the foil are well covered up. You can also use this tip if you want to make large but lightweight beads. The foil will still help you achieve the desired size of the bead you want and maintain your shape, as well as reducing the weight of your bead.

11. To avoid bubbles, put clay fold first into the pasta machine.

Your clay may have bubbles after conditioning it with a pasta machine. Bubbles are not good for clay at all. once your clay starts bringing out bubbles that is a big danger sign. the bubbles are definitely going to expand during baking, and then create an unsightly lump in your work. You can imagine discovering a lump in your work after folding and everything. It will look like a nightmare, but yeah your whole piece is ruined. To avoid such a disaster, insert your folded sheets of clay into the pasta machine fold side first before any other thing. This will prevent your clay from trapping air inside it and having bubbles. If by any means, you still find a bubble in your ball, slice it off using your razor blade, and press out the air by sealing the hole shut with your fingers.

12. You don't need to seal it

Many artists are very sensitive to detail and tend to want to make sure everything is perfect before they go to design. Perfection and accuracy in polymer clay are necessary, but it could become overbearing when you do it too much. Polymer clay is naturally a durable, and water-resistant plastic after baking. The properties in the polymer ensure it remains stable, and strong after baking. Hence, it doesn't need extra efforts or techniques to make it stronger. Neither does it need to be sealed for protection against water. Without any additive or aid, polymer clay itself can withstand water, harsh weather, and last longer than a sealer. The sealer is an artificial toxic chemical that is certain to break down even before the clay will.

Sealers, glazes, and varnishes in themselves can become cloudy or sticky, and begin to peel. It is also susceptible to peel and tear if it comes in contact with harsh brush strokes. This is why you should only use them when you are certain that you truly need them.

Sealers are necessary to use when you use surface embellishments like a metal leaf, foil, or mica powders with your polymer clay. You will need to protect them together. This is where you need a sealer, to hold them together. Also, if there are chances that the acrylic paint you used can be scraped or rubbed off, a sealer is necessary to keep it in place.

However, you also need to be watchful of the type of sealer you purchase. Some sealers do not dry on polymer clay and could end up being sticky. If you are using such a sealer, apply the sealer before baking, so the texture can align well with that of the clay.

13. Follow and obey the dictated baking temperature and time.

Over baking is very consequential and can lead to a change of color. Under-baking can lead to undue breakage.

Polymer clay must be baked properly and accurately for it to be strong and durable.

Under-baking is more consequential and will lead to incomplete or poor curing. Hence, you have to make sure it bakes long enough. It is okay to bake at a temperature a bit higher than the manufacturer's stated temperature.

To protect your project from undue browning, and discoloration, cover your project inside the oven with two aluminum foil pans. This will reduce the effect of the oven's heater on your clay, and prevent the oven from toasting or burning project due to harsh temperatures.

14. Use acrylic paint only

Avoid all manner of gloss or nail polish when doing a final finish on your project. The chemicals in these products are very harsh can dissolve the polymer clay and cause it to become sticky with time. Some of them are very harsh and toxic that they could even go on to melt your clay and soften it. Make sure you go for original acrylic paint, as there are the fake ones that tend to still give the stick effect. Be sure to test your clay with the paint before using it, to ascertain the compatibility. Some clays don't accept acrylic paint. Test your paint with the brand of clay that you are using. Fimo clays commonly have issues with paint, unlike Sculpey that is well adaptive.

15. Get basic tools

So many artists spend so much time trying to get ready for starting polymer craft. You don't need to wait till you hit any jackpot before you start molding. All you need is a pack of clay and your oven.

Every other tool can be improvised with your household tools.

16. Try new things

Do not be afraid to try new techniques in molding your clay project. Let your imaginations be your only limit. You can try combining your clay with other crafts and materials. You can almost never go wrong in polymer craft, as long as you are following the right guidelines. There is no limit to what you can make or achieve with the clay. There are simply no limits. Let your imagination lead you to a new discovery. You might not like what you make but look beyond your errors and let your creativity lead you.

17. To achieve uniformity of lines, designs and details, use the clay extruder.

The clay extruder comes in different packs and styles. For you to achieve a uniform design in your clay products, use a particular set of clay extruder.

18. Knead your clay

You must knead your clay properly before baking. A well-kneaded clay is pliable and soft enough to be molded into any shape of your choice.

Well, it isn't just about the texture but the temperature. kneaded clay is warmer because of the constant contact with your hands. When you knead the clay and make it warm, you are activating the clay and set it alive and ready for work. It is just like you are awaking the clay from slumber.

You don't need to knead your clay like it is flour, you only need to knead it well enough to diffuse air from it and prevent bubbles. Also, you need to knead the clay in small chunks. There is no reason why you should knead the whole pack at once, just tear out a small piece of clay and use the joint of your hands to massage it properly.

19. How do you defeat the lint and dust bunnies?

Dust and dirt bunnies are still possible if your work surface is dusty or dirty. Ensure to wipe down your work surface before you start working or massaging your clay. Also, avoid wiping your hands on your body before working. Lint and dirt could give your work a rough look, asides from that, they affect the texture of your clay and make it less pliable.

Try not to wipe your hands on your pants or other fabrics while working. You might gather dirt particles unknowingly and transfer them to the clay mold you are making. To prevent the temptation of wanting to wipe your hands on your body, keep a neat rag close by for wiping your hands. After wiping your hands, ensure to dust the rag free of any form of particles. To be on a much safer side, use baby wipes to wipe your hands free of lint and particles.

20. To reduce the release of fumes during baking, you can bake clay in sealed bags.

There are several sealed baking bags that you can purchase or improvise. Another alternative is to wash the inside of the oven with baking soda and little water.

21. When you want to improve the texture of the clay mixing.

It increases and sharpens the potential of the project. It can be used to customize color, weight, or stability. You can use Premo as a strong backing or UltraLight for less weight, Glow-In-The-Dark can be mixed with light-colored Scoupely for a ghostly glow. It can be used to increase the glow, color, or texture of the clay.

22. You can formulate your own colors with paint, colored powders, chalk, ink, glitter, colored pencils, powdered makeup and paint.

23. If you don't have access to an oven or yours is quite damaged, and you want to go ahead to bake

your clay, then you should use the Sculpey Air Dry Clay to create quality air-dried projects even without the clay.

A Short message from the Author:

Hey, I hope you are enjoying the book? I would love to hear your thoughts!

Many readers do not know how hard reviews are to come by and how much they help an author.

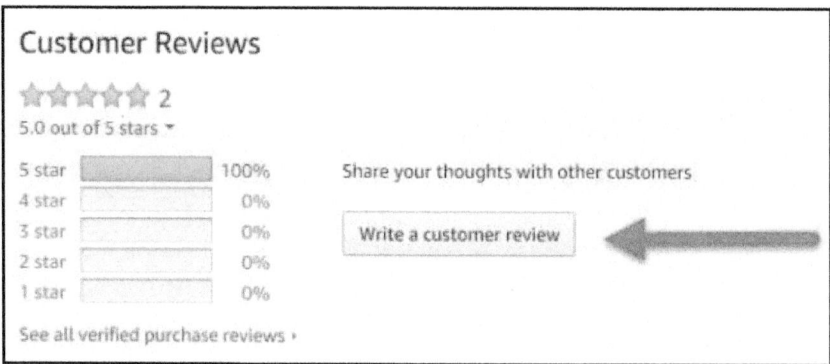

I would be incredibly grateful if you could take just 60 seconds to write a short review on Amazon, even if it is a few sentences!

>> Click here to leave a quick review

Thanks for the time taken to share your thoughts!

Chapter 4

Getting Started with Polymer Clay

Now, we have understood to a great extent the fundamental foundation of polymer clay, let us dig some level deeper. To get started with polymer clay, there are basic tools used in polymer clay craft. There are also safety tips, and items you must familiarize yourself with. We will be discussing them in this chapter.

Basic Tools and Materials

Polymer Clay

There are many forms of polymer clay, each with its distinctive feature. Some are firmer, stronger, and more durable than others. However, they are all still very similar in a way, some of them offer almost the same quality. So, how do you identify unique polymer clays? What features should you look out for when shopping for a particular project?

What kind of polymer clay do I want?

To start this lovely art, you need to get a polymer clay that will allow for versatility, quality, and variety of unique inspiring ideas. The best polymer clay that will satisfy all of these and more is the Sculpey polymer clay. It stimulates imagination like no other clay would, also it fosters creativity and brings artistic vision to life. Others are Fimo and Kato, they also have their unique features.

- Original Sculpey: This is an original clay directly from Polyform products. It works like ceramic clay and easily dries out when exposed to air. It usually has a thick creamy finish, that is very smooth. Sculpey is soft and easily malleable, great for any project you have in mind to do. It is available in two brilliant colors; white and Terra Cotta. This is the most economical choice of polymer, it is also used in classrooms by little children. Most professionals use this for bulkier projects, as it has a great texture that becomes brittle in thin areas after curing. A highly valid polymer clay, the very best there is to use.

- Super Sculpey: This type of polymer clay has almost all the features of the original sculpey but it provides more durability. This clay can be easily carved into complex projects, especially those requiring careful details. It gives premium durability and maximum flexibility. It mostly comes in in pink color, mainly beige pink. It has an amazingly smooth texture that is easy to condition. During conditioning, it tends to ensure fine tooling and proper detailing. A great option for projects with lots of details. Super Sculpey will ensure your product comes out exactly how you want it to.

  However, unlike the original Sculpey, it won't give you a shiny finish. The finish of any product made with Super Sculpey is gross, slightly translucent and matte. Hence, it is mostly used by doll makers and professionals in different spheres of molding. To make the finish appear more interesting, you could add porcelain to it.

- Premo Sculpey: This is another popular strong and durable clay, with an avalanche of beautiful colors. This clay was innovated by curious artists in search of more durable and satisfying polymer clay. They had this idea of a perfect clay and experimented with it, the result of the experiment is the Premo clay. When baking, it might appear stiff at the very first instance but after consistent use, you will get adjusted to its texture, and appreciate its uniqueness. It is a great option for beginners as it has medium firmness and holds fine detail. It is very soft to condition and handle with your hand.

- Sculpey III: This clay is an award-winning children's clay for molding. It comes in a variety of interesting colors, and has a very bright finish, as well as premium softness. You can rightly guess why it is an award-winning children's clay. This clay is very easy for anyone to use, ranging from young children to learning adults. Anyone can make something with this colorful clay. When baked, it becomes very hard and gives a matte, bisque type finish. After curing, you will be amazed at the beautiful appearance of this clay. The texture is a great giveaway.

The Sculpey III maintains tooling, as well as details, and it can be used to make simple jewelry, canes, home décor, and figurines. Finally, it is very versatile and can be mixed with other types of polymer clay to create your own unique, and artistic custom pallet. One clay popularly mixed with the Sculpey is the amazing Premo Sculpey.

Sculpey Super Flex Bake & Bend: This polymer clay also known as "make it and play with it clay" combines the bendability and stiffness quality. It is one of the most malleable or bendable clay after baking, this makes it a perfect choice in molding projects that needs to be posed like dolls. It is a little stiffer than the other clays, but after warming, the conditioning process begins. You can warm with a light bulb. However, after the clay is softened, it becomes very easy to work with.

- Sculpey Ultra-Light: This new clay by Sculpey is always lightweight, easy to handle, and strong after the baking process. It is so light that it can float on water. It is sparingly called the floating clay. You can make floating toys like boats, bath toys, or candle holders. A little of this clay plus any of the other stiff clays like Sculpey Super Flex Bake & Bend could be used to make special projects or ornaments and jewelry. It is also a great choice for papercrafts.

- Sculpey Soufflé: Second to none in jewelry making. Unique for its lightweight after curing, it is just the perfect clay for jewelry making, you wouldn't want to be carrying heavy jewelry on your neck, no matter how beautiful it looks. This is why the Sculpey soufflé is very much outstanding, it allows you to mold the most beautiful lightweight jewelry. The texture is very flexible and holds the tiniest details. You could also use it to perfect your practice or knowledge on the following advanced techniques; modume gane, caning, and bargello. At the end of your molding and baking, you are certain to get a beautifully clean suede finish.

  It is also great for larger projects, as it doesn't break or crack after molding, no matter the size of your project. Yes, it is that strong and self-supporting!

- Translucent Liquid Sculpey: Just as the name depicts, this clay becomes translucent after baking. It comes in a neutral color, hence allowing you to mix in your own desired color powder or paint. It is particularly used as an adhesive between two separate clay products, clay and other surfaces. You could also use it to transfer raw clay to jewelry findings to make a finer mold.

Other none Sculpey polymer clay are:

- Kato Polyclay: This is a professional type of clay with a very tough texture developed by artists for use in complex polymer projects. Due to its tough texture, it is difficult to condition and takes a longer time than other types of polymer clay. It is mostly ideal for holding detail and very sharp lines. If you have hands that tend to leave fingerprints during conditioning, this is a great clay you can use to prevent your hands from leaving fingerprints. It is very solid and great for creating millefiori canes.

After it is baked, it is strong and less flexible than the premo or Souffle clay. It actually comes in very fewer colors than these other brands of clay, but it can be mixed with color or other brands of clay.

- Fimo Professional: This amazing clay comes in only primary colors, hence it is easier to blend colors. It is also a professional clay designed to be well sturdy, stiff and firm. It holds fine details more than any other brand of polymer clay would. It is also very hard to condition and can be very hard at the very first touch. However, all you need is patience, after a little conditioning, the textures begin to relax and in no time you'll enjoy working with this clay. After baking, there is a little alteration to the color, and it is very much firmer and durable.

- Cernit: This colorful clay combines great strength and flexibility to give you a beautiful clay after curing. Its texture is very soft and lightly sensitive to warmer temperatures. It comes in a variety of unique and radiant colors. However, it can also be scarce to find.

Sandpaper

Sandpaper is a special type of modeling tool that allows you to dust off excess clay from your craft. It also allows you to get rid of every form of imperfections left on the surface of your work and gives you a smooth shiny surface. You would find no trace of fingerprints, stains, or unnecessary marks when you use good sandpaper. The best sandpaper to use is the wet/dry sandpaper sheets, it gives the best result there is.

Sculpting Tools

This is a broad category of tools used in shaping your polymer clay. They come in wood, metal or plastic form. The metal ones are most preferred because they are more effective and give perfect effects to your sculpture. Also, they don't build up clay which can lead to drags. There are various types of sculpting tool, just try to discover the one that works for you.

Tissue Blade or Knife

The tissue blade or knife is used to cut out shapes from clay sheets or add fine careful details to your design. The knife tool is very handy for taking out chunks of clay that are in the wrong place, especially tiny places your hand cannot reach. You also need it to easily slice through your work neatly, without causing damage or aberrations to the molding you have achieved already. For this reason, make sure that your knife is sharp, a blunt knife could cause more damage than your hands will. You can also use your kitchen knife if it is sharp, only ensure to wash well immediately after use. Use a long blade knife to prevent distortion or dragging when cutting.

Modeling Tools

These tools are also used in giving detail to the surface of your work. They give the best and minutest detail perfectly even in the smallest nooks. You don't have to use your hands to mess things up when you could simply do that with your modeling tool.

Acrylic Roller

This is used to make your craft flat and smooth. The acrylic role is used to massage the clay until the texture lightens up and the clay is flattened. It should only be used after the clay has been conditioned. After the clay is rolled and well massaged with the acrylic roller, the next step is to start curing and baking. It helps you to flatten your clay well, without it sticking to the roller or the rolling board. It will most definitely leave your work perfectly with no marks.

Skewers

These tools are used to mold polymer clay beads while it is baking. Some persons use a metal knitting needle. It is easy to find, very cheap, and a double-ended metal knitting needle, perfect for skewers. With this tool, you could easily pierce a clay ball of any size and create a perfect hole for your bead. There are different sizes of needles for different types of holes. Slim needles make thin holes; fat needles make fat holes. You could get all the sizes of the needle to be used for a variety of projects. You can bake the clay with the needle pierced into it, and pull it out after it is baked.

Matboard

The matboard is a flat piece of paper used in picture framing, to separate the picture from the glass. It is also used to perform other functions like decorating the picture and adding extra glamor or shine to it.

Oven

Polymer clay can be baked in almost any oven. You don't need to buy any special type of oven to bake this clay. You can use your conventional kitchen oven for baking, only ensure it has good heat control and it has good space for any size of clay. Avoid using small ovens, they could burn your clay faster because their temperature is always extra high, and some of them don't have heat control. Your toaster oven is just perfect for use.

Needle Tool

This is another must-have tool, mostly used in detailing, and punching holes into a conditioned clay. Interesting thing is that it is inexpensive, and you can find it in just any craft store. Yet, it is one highly very valuable tool used to poke, nudge, score, scratch, stipple, and improve the texture of your clay, all to give it a fine finishing.

Pasta Machine

This tool has been mentioned a couple of times in previous chapters. It is used to condition polymer clay, mix colors, smoothen your clay into smooth sheets, and prepare your clay for baking. It relieves you of stress and reduces your work time.

Scissors

After a lump of clay is rolled and baked, it becomes a fine thin sheet of clay that you can cut and use for a uniquely different project. Yeah, that is a possibility you can experiment, remember it is all about creativity.

Setting Up a Polymer Clay Workshop

You actually don't need a ceremonial place to call your polymer clay workshop. Polymer craft can be done in any room where there are space and ventilation. The space is necessary for the storage of tools and mobility. You can dedicate a corner of your house to the curing of polymer clay.

The only scenarios where you will possibly be needing a workshop is if you intend to go full time or big time in polymer clay. You can't afford to be shuttling between your living room, and kitchen in such a case, hence you need to have all your tools set in a particular location.

However, your kitchen or dining area is still a good place. Just ensure that your work area has enough space, and ventilation to make your work comfortable and convenient.

You need a wide, simple table for you to place your clay while you condition it. There are different table options for you to try out, only ensure that your table is well balanced and even with your height, so you won't have to bend so low, or stretch so high while conditioning. After baking in the oven, you can move your clay to a balanced table for drying or finishing.

Polymer Clay Safety Measures

Safety Tips

- Be careful not to burn this clay. The burnt clay will produce an offensive odor that will discomfort you and cause irritation to your breathing passages. Hence, you must be very careful when baking this clay, watch the temperature of the oven, and never leave it on the fire while you wander away. Also, ensure to use a well-balanced oven when baking. It ensures that you gain accuracy in the required temperature of the clay. You can purchase a separate oven thermometer so that you will be able to accurately follow the measurement of heat temperature needed to heat the clay. This is very imperative to avoid burning your clay mistakenly.

- Ensure to keep the polymer clay from the reach of children, if they are not monitored they could throw it into their mouth and cause stomach illness for themselves. It cannot be eaten, though it appears appetizing to the eyes, it could be deadly to the stomach, hence ensure that you keep it away from pets, and little children.
- Make sure your tools are solely dedicated to these purposes, get tools particularly for molding clay and keep it safe. Your tools should be kept safe from the reach of little children or pets. Let your tools be positioned where the hands of little children can't easily bring it down, or where the jaws of your pets won't get to.
- Get latex gloves. A few artists that work with this clay consistently complain of skin irritations. This is not strange because the chemicals in the clay are very harsh.
- If you want to bake for long hours use a vented oven or bake in a separate room with an open window. This is for two valid reasons, one, the bake odor is unpleasant. Second, it is unhygienic. You could get an oven with an exhaust fan. This guide is very imperative to follow if you are

working with any material that has a strong odor, or with a large group of materials.

- You can bake safely in your home ovens, especially if it is well ventilated. You can use a toaster oven.
- It should not be used in anything that will be used for food or cooking. Cookie sheets can be lined used in lining cards during baking. If you use any kitchen item or household tool ensure to wash it well before returning it.
- Keep away from direct sunlight
- Protect your work surface. Cover your work area with wallpaper or foil. This is to prevent the surface area of your work table or furniture from affecting the finish of the conditioned clay.

Basic Polymer Clay Techniques

Most of the techniques used in polymer clay are borrowed from glass making, ceramics, textile, sculpture, and metal making or blacksmithing.

There are different types of techniques for different forms of craft in polymer sculpting. The technique used in jewelry making is way different from the technique used in sculpture or doll making. The required texture and mold are different, so it has to pass through different techniques. However, there are general techniques used in polymer clay crafts, they are listed in detail below.

- Mokume gane: This technique is used in jewelry and sculpture-making to make the clay shiny. To create the shiny effect on your clay, all you need is a blade, needle, ball-tipped tools, a pasta machine, and a sheet of paper to work on.
  - Choose four colors of clay. Make sure that at least one is a metallic clay.
  - Condition all the colors of clay and keep them separately.
  - Pick out things you are going to use to accent your clay, you can use copper leaves and different glitters
  - Put your leafing on your transparent clay alone
  - Choose the clay to add your glitters too, and run them through your pasta machine.
  - Stack them together in any pattern you wish. It is now a loaf.

o Use your roller to flatten the loaf and spread it out.

o Cut your loaf in half, no exact measurement and keep rolling out the clay

o Cut in half and stack the same way. Now you have 32 layers to flatten.

o Roll and flatten, cut in half and restack again.

o Squish the clay into a block and mold with your hands.

o Mold the block carefully until it is perfect.

o Poke the top sides of your mold, using a ball-tipped tool.

o Slice the block vertically in half and poke also.

o Use your blade to create knife signs on top of the block

o Join the two parts together

o Turn the block over and slice lightly with your blade, just as you did earlier.

- Bargello: This technique is unique in itself and also used in making other designs just like mokume gane. To begin, you will have to make a cane and a sheet. You will be needing 3-4 contrasting colors of clay, a pasta machine, a craft knife and a ruler.

- o Condition all your colors of clay and make them into skinner blends using your pasta machine.
- o Fold it in half from color to color
- o Run it through your pasta machine
- o Fold your skinner blend into 1 or 2 folds. Brayer out any bubble or air that shows up between the layers
- o You will have a blended rectangle. Do this for all the colors
- o Slice your stack in slices at approximately 3mm thick.
- o Take the slices and line them up in any order you wish, arrowhead pattern
- o Assemble all the colors together till it forms the arrowhead fully.
- o Reduce it carefully so that the stack of colors blend together. Your bargello design is ready to be used for whatever you wish.

- Conditioning: This is the first technique anybody interested in molding with polymer clay should learn. Conditioning is the process of carefully massaging, and mixing the polymer clay before use. It increases the malleability and strengthens the clay. This process is achieved by consistent kneading and stretching of the clay dough. When the clay is strong and very stiff, you should use a pasta machine in conditioning. During this process, use your hands to roll, knead, stretch the clay until it has the desired texture.

- Baking with polymer clay

  o Each clay varies in baking time, it is usually dependent on the stiffness, texture, alongside other qualities of the clay. The thicker your creation, the higher your baking time. The average baking time for all polymer molds is 275 degrees Fahrenheit for an average of 15 to 30 minutes. Hence, endeavor to always read through the instructions before you resume the baking process, and set your oven heat to the stated temperature.
  o After setting the heat of your oven, preheat the oven before you put the clay.

o It is best not to put your clay directly into the oven in case of spillage. Place the clay on a foil, index card, or ceramic tile, and start to bake.

o After the time given in the instruction pack for baking has elapsed, turn off your oven, and examine your clay. Check the colors, if it has darkened anywhere, then your oven is too hot. Reduce the temperature, and repeat the process again.

o Check at the elapsed time, once your clay is well baked, bring it out of the oven, and allow your clay to cool off before you begin to handle it.

o Once your clay is dry, you can begin to do various designs on it. If you desire a shine, sand it with wet or dry sandpaper under running water, so the particles can fall off freely. Afterward, dry gently with a clean soft cloth.

o To change the color after baking, endeavor to use a glaze or water-based acrylic paint.

- Finishing your creation: After baking, sand and buff your craft once it is cool. You shouldn't work on your baked clay until it is cold to avoid breaking or deforming it. Your finishing can wait till the clay is cold. Once you have sanded and buffed the clay, you can paint it with any color of your choice, and apply a glaze for sealing. Although, it is fine without the glaze. Polymer clay is durable and waterproof, even without a glaze. You can choose to leave the clay the way it is.

- Storing: Truthfully, your polymer clay doesn't air-dry, however, it shouldn't be in the open air for whatever reason. The better the condition you store it, the fresher it remains. Polymer clay is best stored in bags made of polypropylene (PP) plastic. Ensure the place you drop your bag or container after putting the polymer clay in it is dry, and far away from sunlight. Make sure the temperature is no degree above 77 degrees Fahrenheit, and your clay is certain to remain fresh for a long time.

- Making polymer clay hands and feet

    o Make a cylindrical ball of about 1.5 inches long. Make one end a little larger than the rest. It will be used to make the fingers. The smaller end will be used as the wrist.

    o Flatten the larger part so it spreads out like a flat large paddle

    o Use your blade to cut away a little notch on one side

    o Pinch, pull and shape into a thumb. Smooth the round edges using your fingertips and knitting needles

    o Repeat this process until you have all your five fingers ready.

    o Push slightly with your fingers into the middle of the clay to form a cupped hand.

Image Transfer Onto Polymer Clay

For those who can't directly craft designs on polymer clay, image transfer is the alternative way to go about this. There are a hundred ways to do this, and they are all basically simple. You can transfer it directly or make use of specialized products. Here I'll be explaining how you can transfer images to polymer clay using your regular printer. Note that it is only very effective if your clay is white or brightly colored.

- Begin by conditioning your clay, then roll it into a very flat sheet using your pasta machine. Place this sheet on a ceramic tile that you can use to bake. You will be baking the clay sheet on this tile.
- Print out the image from your printer to a manageable size.
- Place the image on the surface of the clay sheet, st exactly where you want the image to be transferred.
- Fold a piece of paper into a small pad, and use it to gently rub the back of your paper against the polymer clay until the paper is in full contact with the polymer clay
- Run the clay and the paper under cold running water. Be careful not to use hot or warm water, as it will smear the image and cause it to disappear.
- Now, use your fingers to rub off the paper from the clay. Do it very lightly in a circular motion, starting at the center so that the image doesn't smear.

- Gently rinse away the paper from the clay, and ensure not to leave any paper left.
- Now you can trim your image on the clay if you wish to. Be careful not to move the image, as any form of slight stretching will distort the image.
- Your clay is ready to be baked. Do not forget to preheat before baking. Avoid touching the surface of the unbaked clay so as not to lose your transferred image.
- After baking, sand the edges using wet-dry sandpaper. Don't sand the surface of the image, you can use a small cloth to buff it lightly. And your clay is ready for use.

Chapter 5

Polymer Clay Project Ideas

Having gone through all the basics and foundational elements of polymer clay, it is time to get your hands busy already. In this chapter, we will be considering 20 polymer clay project ideas you can try out. Some of them are more technical than others, but they are well explained in concise steps and diagrams. We will also be looking at the tools used in making these projects. An oven is a basic supply, you can't make any project outside this supply. So don't expect that it would be mentioned here amongst the tools. If you don't have it, just go ahead and get it, as there is no other alternative.

Let's get into it.

Bangles

If you have a bangle obsession, this is a great project idea for you to try as a beginner. With very simple steps, you can make your own bangles, as many as you want. Here is a simple step by step guide on how to make your own bangles. To get started, you need

- Various colors of polymer clay
- A metal bracelet
- A knife or cutting tool
- A scissors

Procedures

Step 1: Use your knife to cut a thin lump of polymer clay. Don't make it too thin, so it won't break when you are rolling it.

Step 2:

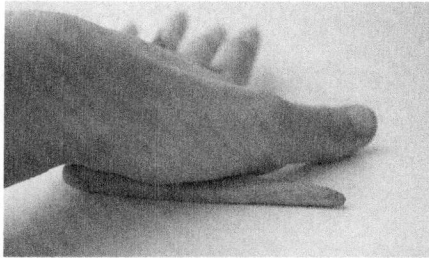

Use the palm of your hand to roll it in such a way that the lump is thick and round.

Step 3: Do the same for all your colors of polymer clay for as many bangles as you want.

Step 4:

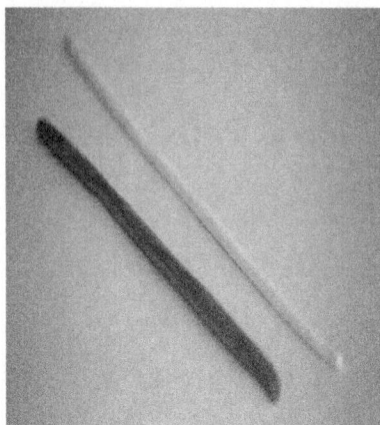

Twist two lumps of different colors together by wrapping one over the other. You could twist lumps of the same color together, the idea is to make it thick, nothing more. Don't overstress the clay, make the twist or wrap as careful as possible.

Step 5:

Use your palm to roll them on together lightly to get them to blend properly.

Step 6:

Here is where we use the metal bracelet, you are going to use it as a guideline to measure and shape our DIY bangle well before it kisses the oven. Wrap your DIY bangle around the bracelet, and cut out the excesses using scissors.

Step 7: Mush the rough ends of the bangle together so they appear well intertwined. Use your fingertips to smooth it out well.

Step 8: Remove the bracelet, and place your bangle or bangles in the oven to bake. Set your temperature at 275 degrees, and allow it to bake for 20 minutes.

Note: You could bake your bangles one after the other, but when baking them at the same time, be careful that they don't touch each other.

Your Bangles are ready!

Round Bead Necklace

Here is one interesting project you are going to be thrilled you tried. I know it looks quite complicated, but it is basically simple and easy. You just need a little confidence and a little persistence, and yes, you can do it. Here is a brief list of what you need to get started;

- Various colors of polymer clay
- Waxed cotton cord
- Toothpick

Procedures

Step 1: Begin by conditioning your clay, each pack at a time. Massage them carefully until they are soft and pliable.

Step 2: Cut small parts of the conditioned clay, and roll them in between your palms until they are round. Make little balls by rolling this clay with the palm of your hand. You can make various sizes of these clay balls, but ensure that they are consistent. There should be more than one ball representing each size of ball you make.

Step 3:

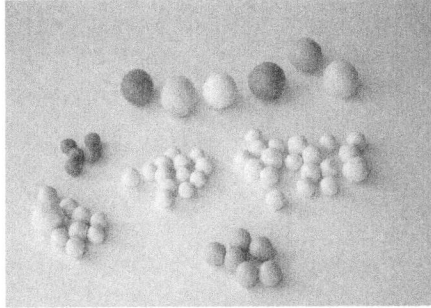

Repeat the two steps for all the colors. Feel free to play with colors and gather as many colors as you wish, only ensure that they are all matching. You don't want to wear a color masqueraded jewelry; three to four colors are sufficient.

Step 4:

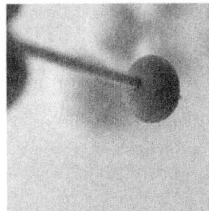

Next, you use your toothpick to poke a tiny hole in the center of each bead. Don't exert too much pressure on the balls so as not to destroy their already round shape. Make the holes large enough for the string you want to use to hold the beads together. You can wear latex gloves on your hands to avoid smooching the clay ball with fingerprints marks.

Step 5: Place the beads on a baking tray and let them bake for 25 minutes at 270 degrees.

Step 6: At the elapsed time, bring out your beads to prevent them from burning and string them together. You can make it as long as you want.

Step 7: Attach closure at the end to keep the beads from falling out. You can make as many necklaces as you want. Your necklace is ready to be rocked!

Geometric Bead Necklace and Bangle

Wondering what this means? This means other shapes asides the common circle. There are other forms of bead necklaces you will definitely love to try. And guess what? I'll be teaching you basic tricks to create other shapes of necklaces. With these tips, you can create any other shape of your choice. To make this unique type of necklace, you need to get the following tools:

- Polymer clay block
- Razor blade
- Cord, lace cord preferably
- Toothpick
- Magnetic closure

Procedures

Step 1: knead your clay and massage it well until it is soft and pliable.

Step 2:

Cut and roll as many balls as you wish, again you can make different sizes of clay balls.

Step 3: Use your razor blade to cut little pieces off each clay ball to give you a geometric shape. Make sure to carve carefully around the clay ball. For other types of shapes, you can also use your blade to carve the clay ball. However, make sure to cut and carve carefully so that your clay ball or mold still retains its thickness and texture. There is no limit to the shapes you can make, you can carve out a star, heart shape, triangle and others.

Step 4:

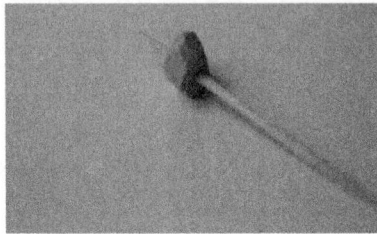

Poke a hole in the middle of the clay ball using your toothpick.

Step 5: Put into an oven and bake for 15 minutes at 275 degrees.

Step 6: Thread your beads through with the lace cord, and attach the magnetic closure at the back. Tie the two ends together before attaching the magnetic closure.

Your bangle is ready!

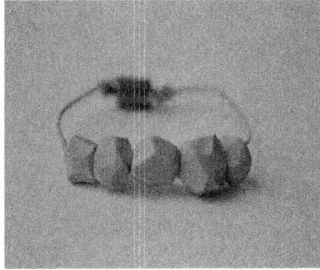

Braided Bracelet

Here is another amazing project for you to try. Yeah, another bracelet! But a lovelier one. This braided bracelet is pretty easy to make. You can get your bracelet done in just an hour. I assure you, it is no hard work, just ensure you follow the process. You require only the following tools:

- Polymer clay
- Razor blade

Procedures

Step 1:

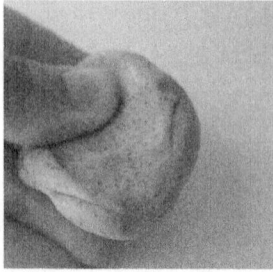

Knead your clay gently till it is softened up.

Step 2:

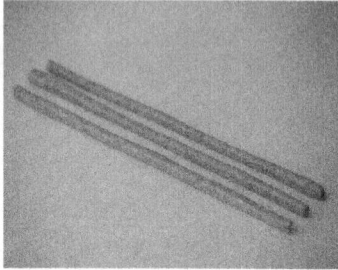

Divide the clay with your hands into three equal pieces. Roll each of them using your palm. Roll gently and carefully till you have three thin long tubes.

Step 3:

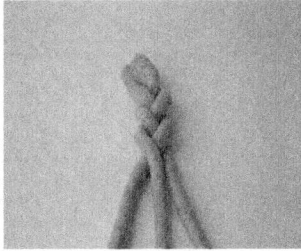

Join the tips of the three tubes together by mashing them. After that, start braiding like the picture shows. Place each of the tubes over each other one after the other.

Step 4: Braid to your desired length, you can measure using your hands till you feel the length is accurate.

Step 5:

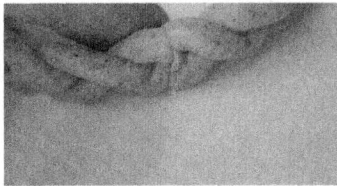

Use your blade to cut the two ends, and join them together by gently pressing them against each other.

Step 6: Your bracelet is ready to be baked. Bake for 25 minutes at 245 degrees.

You don't need a cord. Your bracelet is as good as done!

Rose Earrings

These projects will get you obsessed with polymer clay forever. No hypes. It looks technical, but if you ask me, I'll tell you the steps are just interesting. It is very inspirationally amazing and will birth other awesome ideas in your head. Here is a short list of what you need to get:

- Polymer clay
- Razor blade
- Earposts and backs
- Glue, preferably krazy glue

Procedures

Step 1: Roll out six little balls of clay.

Step 2: Use your hands to flatten them out, so that it expands and stays flat. Don't make it too thin though.

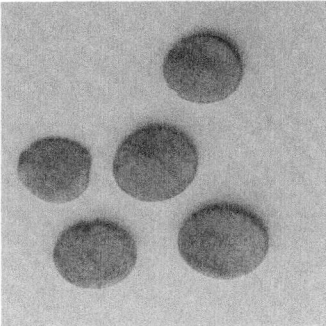

Step 3:

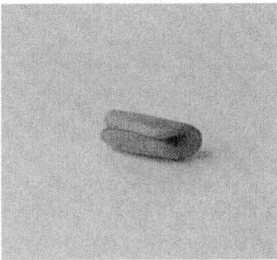

Take one of the flattened clay and fold it in, so that one of the ends closes the fold and it has a cylindrical shape. This will be used to form the center of the rose.

Step 4:

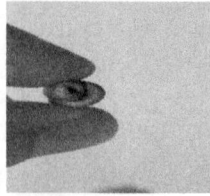

Place the other flattened balls around the folded ball. Let them stick to the flattened clay well. They will be the petals.

Step 5: Slice the end of the rose off, so we can have a very flat end to place the earring post.

Step 6:

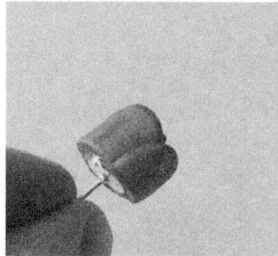

Okay, I just mentioned the earring post. Here is where we use it. Stick the rose to the earring post.

Step 7: Place the pair on a baking tray and bake for 15 minutes at 275 degrees.

Your amazing earrings are ready!

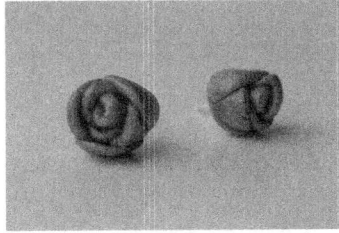

Indian Inspired Necklace

This necklace is culturally worn in India, but thanks to globalization, you can own a pair now. Well, not just own a pair, you can actually make a pair yourself now! Isn't that just awesome? To make this amazing necklace, you need;

- As many-colored polymer clay blocks as you want.
- Leather cord
- Razor blade
- Magnetic closure
- Toothpick

Procedures

Step 1:

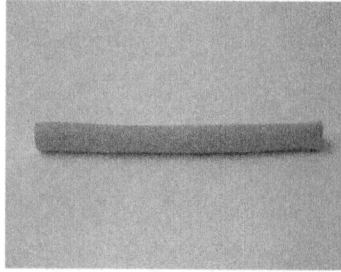

Roll a lump of clay into a thin tube.

Step 2:

Slice the tube into different sizes of beads. They should all still look long and straight.

Step 3:

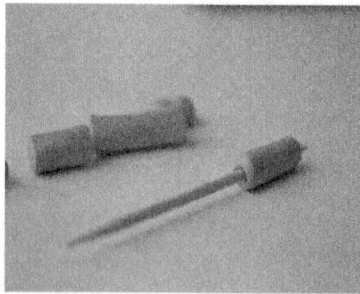

Poke a hole using your toothpick in each bead.

Step 4: Cut as colored many beads as possible, in measurement with the length of necklace you want to make.

Step 5:

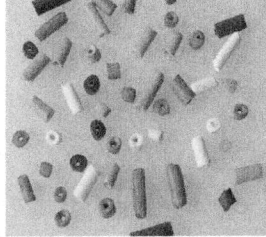

When you are done cutting, put all the beads on the baking tray. Insert into your oven, and bake at 275 degrees for 15 minutes.

Step 6: Let your beads cool, and string them all into the cord.

Step 7: Attach your magnetic closure, and your necklace is ready to wear.

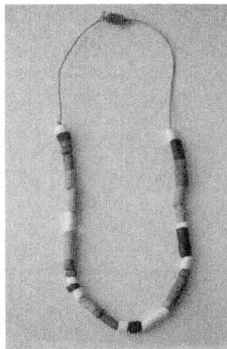

Gumball Garland

This classic project idea is an all-timer. You can try it with little kids, I don't need to tell you how easy it is. Do I? well, the only stress probably in this project is having to make repeated balls of the same size. As I already mentioned, you can use the help of little children. They don't have to be professionals; you can guide them through it. So, if a child can do this, I don't know why you can't. Okay, too much talk. Let's get into this already.

Here is a brief list of what you need to get started.

- An assortment of polymer clay
- Waxed cotton cord
- Toothpick

Procedures

Step 1: Start by conditioning your balls. You need your balls to be really soft, so give a few more minutes to conditioning and kneading this clay.

Step 2:

Decide on the size of your garland. Rip small chunks of clay, and start rolling them into round balls. Do these for all the colors you decided to use.

Step 3:

Once you are done making as many assorted balls of your choice, poke a hole in each of these folded balls using the toothpick. Guide the children to make the holes at the center, and not at the sides. (if you have them as aides)

Step 4: Place all your clay balls in the oven and bake for 30 minutes at 275 degrees.

Step 5:

Now, string them into your waxed cotton cord in color pattern, just like we have in the pictures.

You can hang this garland just anywhere.

Cat Sculpture

And here is our first sculpture. Yeah, we were coming to this point from the jumbles of jewelry projects. We will still have a look at some amazing jewelry projects but let's take a break from that stuff for now. This is a great project to challenge yourself with as a beginner, and nah you don't need to be intimidated at all, it is just folding, rolling, and bending. It is basically an extension of some of the techniques that are being used in jewelry making, which you should be familiar with by now.

So, here is what you need:

- A pack of polymer clay (Sculpey Souffle preferably)

- Plain paper
- A sheet of printer paper
- Paperclips
- A little bottle of alcohol
- A knife

Procedures

Step 1: The Sculpey soufflé is too soft to use straight from the pack. Hence you have to reduce the oil in it using a plain sheet of paper to soak the oil out.

Step 2:

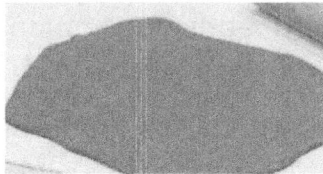

Flatten a very large chunk on top of a printer sheet of paper. Place another sheet on the clay and press it into the clay, so it is as flat as possible.

Step 3: You can leave the clay for a day so it is much firmer to use. Roll a large lump of clay into a big ball, then divide it in the middle. One of the sides will be used for the top bun of the hamburger. For the lower part, cut the other side of the bun into half, so there is just a little part left.

Step 4: Mash a small ball of clay and place it between the lower and upper bun.

Step 5:

Make multiple small cheese balls, and stick them around the bun. These balls should look like bubbles. They will be used to make the cheeseburger.

Step 6: You are making one hamburger and one cheeseburger. Repeat steps three and four to make the buns of the hamburger. The hamburger would have lettuce spilling out of it from the sides. The second one will look bitten off. To create biting marks, use a straw to make biting marks on the clay.

Step 7: You need a smooth surface for the clay. To achieve this, dip your paintbrush into alcohol and use it to touch the round sides of the clay until it is smooth.

Step 8:

Cut out another lump of clay and roll it up to form a cylindrical or spherical shape. Place this lump on the hamburger.

Step 9:

Stretch the four edges so there is a straight line showing on them. Pierce two holes on both sides of the front part of the clay.

Step 10: you can bake this sculpture for 45 mins at 150 degrees.

Step 11: Paint the parts of this sculpture with different bright colors. Indicate the eyes of the cat using black paint. Use paperclips to make the whiskers.

Your sculpture is ready.

Flower Sculpture

This is one simple sculpture you can make in a very short time. The flower is made in such a way that you can attach anything to it to make it visible. Here is what you need to get started.

- Two colors of Polymer clay

Procedures

Step 1: Take a chunk of clay and massage it carefully with your hands. Continue massaging it until it is soft enough to mold.

Step 2: Take a color of polymer clay and roll it into a small ball.

Step 3: Press your hands into the ball, to create a compression. That would be the middle point of the flower.

Step 4: Make round balls of the second color of polymer clay, and make a compression like you did in the previous step, but make a little drag from the middle point of the compression to one side of the ball.

Step 5: Shape the side of the mold so that it is well pointed and uniform with one another.

Step 6: Place them around the first impressed ball and mash them on it.

Step 7: You can repaint the mold for a shinier look. Bake in the oven for 20 minutes at 200 degrees.

Your flower sculpture is ready!

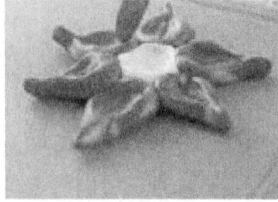

Vessel Sculpture

This sculpture is basic and very easy to make. It looks tribal, can't really say what tribe owns this cultural piece, but this piece is very homely. One you will be proud of having in your house as decoration.

- Clay
- Newspaper
- Water
- Fork, knife, spoon
- Paintbrush
- Paint
- Rolling pin

Procedures

Step 1: Knead the clay with your palms until the texture is even.

Step 2: Use your rolling pin to roll the clay flat on the paper.

Step 3: Pick up the clay and roll it into a round ball.

Step 4: Press your fingers into the clay ball to create an impression that looks like a ball. Keep punching and pulling the bowl until the shape is satisfying.

Step 5: Cut small chunks of clay and roll them into long tubes.

Step 6: Coil the tube carefully so that you have perfect coils.

Step 7: Stack the coils together by joining them at the corners to create a vessel.

Step 8: Roll out another lump of clay until the whole lump is even height.

Step 9: Cut out the bottom of the clay and divide the lump into equal parts.

Step 10: Join the coils, clay bowl together.

Step 11: Bake your clay vessel in the oven for 35 minutes at 250 degrees.

Step 12: You can paint it with any color of your choice.

Your vessel is ready!

Gold Bar Beads

This project is uniquely to teach you how to change the color of polymer clay successfully. Not just to change the color of polymer clay but to make it shiny and appear very real. Yes, so this project requires:

- Translucent polymer clay
- Gold powdered pigment
- Razor blade
- Toothpick
- Waxed cotton cord

Procedures

Step 1: Cut a little chunk of clay and massage it between your palm

Step 2:

Pour the gold pigment into a bowl. Put the clay into the bowl and roll it with the gold pigment so that it is well coated. Massage the clay and dip it into the bowl to coat it with the gold pigment again. repeat the process until the clay is now a vibrant shade of gold.

Step 3: Roll your lump of clay into a thin thread.

Step 4: Cut out the rough edges and roll out every imperfection using the razor blade.

Step 5: Use your toothpick to create a hole inside the thread. Dust some gold pigment on the clay one last time to ensure it has a beautiful shine.

Step 6: Place in the oven and bake for 15 minutes at 250 degrees.

Step 7: String your cotton cord through and tie the ends together.

Heart Earrings

Here is another simple project with straightforward steps and memorable guidelines. All you need to make this project are:

- Red polymer clay
- A heart cut out
- Earring post and backs
- Glue

Procedures

Step 1: Massage the clay in between your hands so that they are pliable and easy to manipulate

Step 2: Cut out an even piece of clay, and roll it with a clay roller.

Step 3:

Place your heart cutout on the clay and make two hearts. Use your blade and pencil to get the heart out of the clay lump.

Step 4: Bake in an oven for 15 minutes at 230 degrees.

Step 5: Glue the heart to the earring post.

Your earring is ready to flaunt.

Gift Tags

This is an awesome gift idea to give to your family and loved ones.

Here's a brief list of what you need to make this awesome project:

- Polymer clay
- Acrylic paint
- Flat wooden sticks
- Rolling pin
- Fat needle
- Paintbrush
- Crochet thread
- Cookie cutters of different shapes; star, heart, cloud, geometry, etc.

Procedures

Step 1: Soften a piece of clay by kneading it repeatedly.

Step 2: Roll the clay on the flat tile using the rolling pin. Roll the clay until it is very flat.

Step 3:

Make several cuts of different shapes using the cookie cutter.

Step 4: Before stamping your clay, dry the metal stamp tool with a cloth to make sure it is dry.

Step 5:

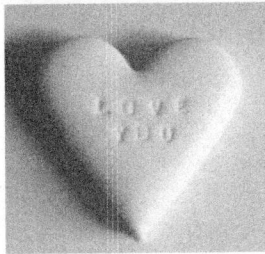

Hold the tool properly and press it into the clay.

Step 6: Take the clay off the tile and punch a hole through to the backside using the fat needle.

Step 7: Preheat the oven to 110 degrees and bake the clay for 30 minutes. Put the clay in the oven with the tile.

Step 8:

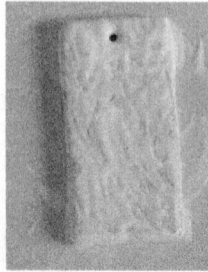

Put some acrylic paint on the paper plate and paint the front and edges of the clay plate.

Step 9: Leave it to dry for a while.

Step 10:

After a short while, rub off the paint with some damp cloth. Most of the paint will go off.

Step 11:

Pass the crochet through the hole at the top and wrap it around your gift parcel.

Your metal letter set is ready for use.

Pendant

Are you a lover of simple necklaces? This amazing pendant can be used on any type of necklace. It costs you a lot cheaper than purchasing one out there. So let's get into it already.

You need,

- Metallic spray paint
- Clear gross polyurethane
- Necklace chain
- Jump ring and a clasp
- Needle and pen

Procedures

Step 1: Massage a small lump of clay briefly

Step 2: Roll it into small balls

Step 3: Use a min rolling pin to flatten it out a bit

Step 4:

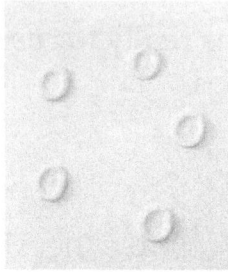

Press your smallest finger into the clay

Step 5:

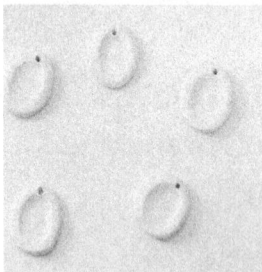

Use your needle to make a little hole at the top for the chain to pass through. Let the hole be moderate; not too thin and not too fat.

Step 6: Place the clay in an oven and bake for 15 minutes at 275 degrees.

Step 7: Spray the cured clay with clear gross polyurethane and allow to dry.

Step 8: Attach the jump ring to your pendant and pass your necklace through the ring.

Your pendant necklace is very ready! Who knew it could be this easy?!

Snowman Ornament

Here is another interesting project for you to try. It proves to be fun and is very much easy to do. You can teach this project to a small child and watch them create magic. Most interestingly, it doesn't require so much to make.

Here is a brief list:

- Polymer clay (white, black, blue, orange and other colors)
- Cute little thumbs
- String or ribbon

Procedures

Step 1: Cut and roll three even balls of white clay.

Step 2:

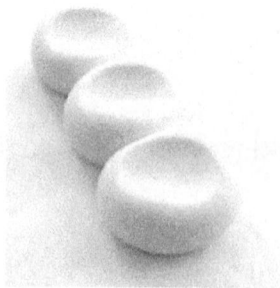

Join them together in a string manner, and cause an impression in each of the clay by pressing your thumb into the clay.

Step 3:

You'll need to make tiny balls of black clay for the eyes, a cone roll of orange clay for the nose.

Step 4: Make a thin long tube of blue clay, you can insert jewelry wire into the roll to make it flexible for the snowman ribbon.

Step 5: Place the round black clay for the eye, and three on the body of the clay. Place the orange mold in the middle of the first clay. Also, wrap the ribbon around the intersection of the first and second clay. Be careful not to smooch the clay.

Step 6: Bake this snowman at 270 degrees for 20 minutes.

Step 7: You can put a jump ring at the top and use it for decorations.

Your snowman is ready!

Buttons

These beautiful buttons don't stress a muscle to make. They are basically easy and basic. We will be using the same steps we used in bead making, the only difference is that you don't have a round shape here, but a flat circular shape. Note, if you want a design like the one you have on the colorful button, you have to first make mokume game techniques and other techniques to make colorful buttons like this. However, all you need are;

- A pack of clay of different colors
- A needle or toothpick
- A round cutter (like the one used in making the gift tags)

Procedures

Step 1: Roll your clay into a flat shape after massaging it. roll it flat to your desired texture, make it just as flat as you want it to be.

Step 2: Use the round cutter to make cuts of circular round shape.

Step 3: Pass the toothpick through the flat clay in two places to make button holes

Step 4: Bake the clay at 250 degrees for 20 minutes.

Step 5: Leave it to cool. Your buttons are ready.

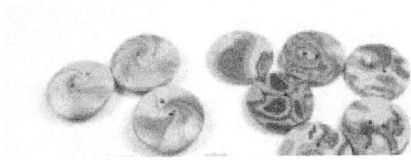

Tortoise

As complex as this project looks, it might happen to be the most interesting project you would ever try. You will need;

- Two colors of polymer clay (one dark and one light color)
- Rolling pin

Procedures

Step 1: Roll the light-colored clay into a ball. It will be the base of the tortoise.

Step 2: Flatten it slightly.

Step 3: Make four little balls of the same color to make the hands and legs of the tortoise.

Step 4: Flatten all the balls, the smaller ones would be for the legs and the longer ones will be for the hand. Attach them to the base.

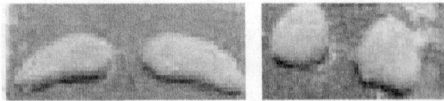

Step 5: Mold a round ball for the head, and attach it.

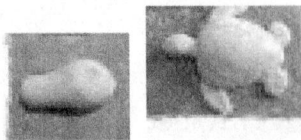

Step 6: Use the darker color of clay to make cracked shells like shown in the picture.

Step 7: Bake in the oven for 25 minutes at 275 degrees.

Step 8: You can apply glaze or varnish to give it a glowing shine.

Your sculpture is done!

Twin Doll

This twin doll is simply amazing. It is basically interesting and challenging. You will need;

- Three colors of polymer clay
- Marker

Procedures

Step 1: Make two circles using two different colors

Step 2: Make a cuboid mold

Step 3: Make indentions on the circle you made in step one using a color for the nose and use the marker to make marks for the eyes.

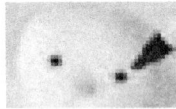

Step 4: Put the toothpick into the cuboid.

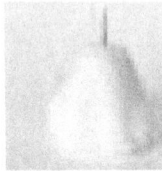

Step 5: Pass the head into the cuboid through the toothpick.

Step 6: Repeat the process to make a second doll.

Step 7: Roll out a thin rod of clay for the tails.

Step 8: Shift the two dolls close to each other and cross the tails.

Step 9: Bake for 20 minutes at 280 degrees. Be careful not to scatter the mold as you move it into the oven.

Your doll is ready

Dragon

This dragon toy is a very beautiful gift your child or loved one will desire to have.

It could be a little tricky but you will thrive on this so, nothing to fear. For this, you will need;

- Spine
- Two colors of polymer clay
- Rolling pin

Procedures

Step 1: Select an armature of your choice, and prepare a log of clay.

Step 2: Flatten the log and press onto the armature

Step 3: Enclose the armature and blend the edges to make the body pose.

Step 4: Blend the tail to fit the body pose

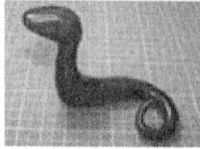

Step 5: Take a different color and make two circles.

Step 6: Cut two feet, and make out three toes. Also, cut out a plate shape for the chest region using a different color of clay.

Step 7: Attach all the pieces to the body.

Step 8: Roll out two logs for the hand, and cut out three fingers. Attach it to the body.

Step 9: Make circles for the eyes and spikes for the back.

Step 10: Make horns and spikes on the head.

Step 11: Make wings with the two colors of clay.

Step 12: Attach wings and bake for 30 minutes at 270 degrees.

Step 13: You can apply glaze or varnish for a shiny finish.

Clay Bird

Okay, here is one basic one. I know I have used the word basic a couple of times, but trust me you cannot mess up this one. It has very straight forward steps that anyone can scale through.

All you need to make this are;

- Polymer clay
- Tooth pick
- Black paint

Procedures

Step 1: Massage a lump of clay until is very soft and pliable.

Step 2: Roll the lump into a ball

Step 3: Make a cone shape from the ball, like that of ice cream.

Step 4: Draw out the top part of the ice cream, to make a pointed mouth

Step 5: Smoothen the bottom to make it flat enough for standing

Step 6: Make a pointed shape on the top circular part, and mark out the beak

Step 7: Use the toothpick to create details on the bird, you could also use it to perfect the shape of the clay.

Step 8: You can bake the clay already

Step 9: Paint your bird with your desired color, and paint the beak black

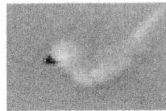

Chapter 6

Common Polymer Clay Mistakes to Avoid

Making mistakes as a beginner could be inevitable, but sometimes they could be highly consequential. You cannot just avoid mistakes by being careful, the hard truth is that no matter how hard we try, we can't always beat making mistakes. Mistakes happen in life, art and polymer clay. There are some tips you need to keep at your fingertips, and some mistakes, in particular, you have to beware of.

A brief list has been compiled for you to engage in. Ensure to go through them carefully, if possible more than once, so you familiarize yourself with them and get your fingers equipped with a good bank of knowledge on what you need to do.

Many persons start their modeling career with polymer clay like it is just any clay, even though you have been molding all your life, you could still fall for all these highly consequential mistakes.

There are pitfalls to be avoided. As a beginner, you are very much advantaged to be aware of this. It will save you a lot of trouble and errors.

1. Have you ever had the terrifying imagination of how possible it is to smash your whole sculpture after making it? Yeah, no one plans to do that but it is one thing that is most certainly possible when you are making large sculptures and you are not so careful. It doesn't take so much to smash a project as much as it takes incredibly long hours to make them. hence, you have to be consciously careful.

2. Failure to fully condition your clay: This mistake is particularly common amongst beginners. Sometimes, they could wrongly assume that a clay lump is soft after rolling it through their palms a few times. No professional would make such a costly assumption. Every form of clay needs to be well conditioned and massaged, even though the description says "soft".

3. Failure to clean your work surface: This is a common mistake amongst first-time artists as

well. They could be very forgetful and tend to leave the table uncleaned. No matter the dose of excitement bubbling over the new project you are doing, you still have to retain a consciousness of your work environment. Clay is very sensitive to lint, dust, dirt, and water. No matter how much hurry you are in, or excitement you have got, take out the few minutes to wipe your work surface clean. It is also necessary you clean your hands. No matter how clean they appear, clays with light colors like white or yellow can easily detect dirt and adjust to it. This invincible dirt could end up giving your work dirt streaks. So before working with polymer clay, ensure to wash your hands very well, and also don't forget to clean under your fingernails. Dirt could slip from your nails into the clay mold.

4. Failure to pre-heat your oven: Although, this is not commonly preached. It is something you should do. I am trying to be careful and not use the must word. But I actually believe that you must pre-heat the oven before baking. It helps to stabilize the temperature of the oven before your

clay goes into it. Also, it helps to increase the strength and stamina of your pieces and curtail the spikes. A curtailed and regulated oven will produce a well-cured clay. Preheating your oven ensures that your clay bakes at the correct temperature for the correct period. Heat mistakes like burning, scorching, and others can be avoided if your oven is preheated. Yes! it can be so helpful.

5. Being stereotyped: Many beginner artists usually mold clay just the way they saw it in the guideline, with no innovations, spices, or additions. This is very bad for polymer clay because this art is all about creativity and innovations. Even when you are following a pattern or design, feel free to add your own expressions to it. Feel free to experiment with different shapes and with different colors. Be limitless because you actually are.

6. We don't know when to stop: Okay, it is one thing to be stereotyped, and another to be excessively detailed. Imagine a craft with so

many details in one place, that will be yuck! It could distract you from the main point of the whole design if there is any. Know when to put a full stop to the creativity. Know when it is time to stop adding anything in total. You need to know when it is time to drop your pencils.

7. Spending to get expensive materials: Some artists wrongly believe that they must have all the tools ready before they can start molding. They believe that the more complicated your tools are, the greater the sign of your readiness to begin working or molding.

8. Failure to enjoy the process: So often spend so much energy on trying to make the project clay and trying to perfect it, that we fail to improve our exposure. Also, you fail to enjoy the process, as your whole mind is fixed on how to make it perfect. Hence, it is also important that you consciously call yourself back and focus on both the friends.

9. Failure to test products yourself: So many artists are afraid of testing their projects themselves, and solely rely on the testimony of others who have taken the pain to do the product test themselves. Testing the product yourself allows you to fully understand the properties of the clay. Also, you know the type of designs you would want to do, so you must test the clay yourself to ascertain its texture.

10. Never investing in a class tutorial or book: There is indeed a lot of good free information on the internet for learning polymer clay. If you type a question on polymer in google, you are certain to get answers in minutes. However, there are special blogs and training sites you have to pay for. Yes, there will be free stuff all the time, you can't compare the result of advanced learning with free classes.

11. Not making time to create: The above leads right into this. Sometimes for whatever reason, we could just procrastinate and procrastinate when we are going to make that polymer project. Save

screenshots after screenshots on social media, and go on ahead. However, making screenshots of projects and failing to do them is a crazy trend that must end. No matter how skeptical you are, you have to first give it a try.

12. Using weak polymer clay for thin pieces: When making a thin plastic stick, you must pay much attention to the texture of your clay, and how thick it is. Your polymer clay must be thick when you are making a thin piece project. Ensure that the mixture maintains its strength and stability. Also, bake it for a longer time to make it hard and sturdy. Under-baked thin polymer clay will not only crumble but one day it could break and shatter completely. Hence, you have to bake your clay for at least 30 minutes.

Also, you need to be careful to ensure that you are using the right brand of polymer clay for your project. Some clays are sturdier and stronger than others. So, be sure that the clay you are using is one that has great strength.

13. Under-baking polymer clay: Polymer clay is made from PVC powder, and other stuff like plasticizers, binders and fillers, lubricant, and pigments. After baking, the clay absorbs harsher temperatures during curing. And when a clay is not well baked, the clay will fail to fuse together, and then the fusion becomes incomplete and could lead to the whole piece of clay falling apart. An unbaked polymer is susceptible to breaking and crumbling. They might even remain sticky after days of work and extraordinarily soft. Hence, you must ensure that you bake much and you don't know that you baked for long in one place. use an oven thermometer to measure the temperature so you can accurately bake your plastic and give it the right texture it needs.

14. Overbaking polymer clay: This occurs when you leave the clay in the oven far beyond the required baking time or with an aggressive temperature. Polymer clay usually starts to burn when it reaches temperatures near 350°F (176°C). Some brands of polymer clay can be highly sensitive and could burn if you leave it long even at a

lower temperature. Some people wrongly believe that baking for a longer time at a lower temperature will take care of the consequences of overbaking. Lowering your temperature and extending your work time could give you an under-baked work. Accuracy in baking isn't necessarily about the baking time, but the temperature used in baking. Hence, you must pay more attention material.

15. Using nail polish as a polymer clay glaze: Some internet artists do tutorial videos where they use nail polish as a clay glaze. It always comes out looking really shiny and beautiful like you could actually grab it and rub it against your cheeks. Like, it appears really cute. The whole thing seems like a really good idea, and you are beginning to consider trying it. Well, sorry to burst your bubbles, it is not. Nail polish is one of the worst things you can ever use as a glaze of varnish for finishing your clay mold. It could turn sticky and goopy over time, but well the video won't show you that. I would advise you not to bother wasting your time on an already failed

experiment. You should use a proper clay sealer than finding alternatives to it.

16. Using a spray varnish on polymer clay: They are some spray varnish that doesn't align well with polymer clay. The problem with all these sealers and glazes is that they tend to turn really sticky overtime. The sadder news is that some of them don't dry. They will remain sticky and gooey over time. Have in the corner of your mind that what works with one type of clay might not work well with another.

Well, you can save your clay mold if the varnish happens to be unapologetically sticky. Use 91% isopropyl alcohol to remove sticky spray sealers. Like they will help you to totally get rid of them.

17. Storing polymer clay open to the air: A common beginner mistake that could cost you an extra dollar to get a new clay pack. Exposing your clay to the open air is very wrong and could lead to early damage. The air dries the clay over time and it becomes very hardened. This is why polymer clay must be stored in airtight containers to help

retain the moisture and grant your polymer clay long-lasting freshness throughout the years. Storing it in an open place could also cause it to come in contact with a lot of lint and dirt that makes it inconvenient for use. Safe storage isn't just to help the texture but the freshness and usability of the clay.

18. Embedding eye pins without a kink: When you make polymer clay pendants or charms, you'll want to include a hanging loop at the surface. Most artists just take the commonly available jewelry eye pin, adjust the length, and insert it into the raw clay. But after baking, it doesn't stay in, the wire of the eye pin pulls out of the clay. Some artists usually glue the pin and adjust it back into the baked clay. This is not always sturdy and could break out.

The best way is to create a small kink at the top or bottom end of the eye pin before embedding it into the raw clay. This way it cannot pull out after curing. The lesson here is; always put a kink or bend in your eye pin before inserting it into polymer clay.

19. Using the wrong glue with polymer clay: Glue is a great aid in polymer claying, it acts as a great adhesive to hold clay in place with other decorative pieces or accessories. In erring making, the glue is sometimes used to hold the ear post to the earring. Hence you have to be careful to get a really good glue that will hold everything sturdy. However, just like the problem with paint or varnish, you can't really tell a good glue by looking at it. And no one glue can glue everything in place. Some glues are more effective in gluing only some type of attachments. Superglue is very flexible and can be used in holding almost anything in place but it holds clay to metal best. Another recommended glue that can be used on metal jewelry is the E6000 glue. However, it sticks with wood or paper better. Baked bond seems to be the strongest there is. It holds polymer clay to polymer clay and other hard substances.

20. Smashing your clay mold: I would advise that after making every huge piece and mashing it with the other part, place it in the oven. You don't

have to bake the whole piece at once. You might be worried about how you will mash them altogether if you mold and bake them individually. Well, after baking, it takes polymer clay about 15 minutes to be fully cured. So, within that time, you can still join your individual parts together. Also, if you don't want to go through this method, only ensure that your clay is kept in place after molding to prevent you from smashing the whole edifice with your hands.

21. The wrong pen for drawing on polymer clay: One of the wrong pens you can ever use are solvent-based, dye-based markers. These markers are very flexible and are used for all manner of beautiful art. But it is a bad choice for drawing on polymer clay, as the dye tends t diffuse into the clay, and create a blur or bleed effect. The best pen you should use on your polymer clay is the pigment-based marker. There are so many brands you can choose from. Those are the best pen you can use in drawing.

The end... almost!

Hey! We've made it to the final chapter of this book, and I hope you've enjoyed it so far.

If you have not done so yet, I would be incredibly thankful if you could take just a minute to leave a quick review on Amazon

Reviews are not easy to come by, and as an independent author with a little marketing budget, I rely on you, my readers, to leave a short review on Amazon.

Even if it is just a sentence or two!

So if you really enjoyed this book, please...

>> Click here to leave a brief review on Amazon.

I truly appreciate your effort to leave your review, as it truly makes a huge difference.

Chapter 7

Polymer Clay Frequently Asked Questions (Q&A)

As a first time user of polymer clay, it is must certain that you would have some doubts that need to be cleared, and information to aid your use of polymer clay. Check them out below.

Question: Can I paint polymer clay?

Answer: Most definitely, yes! But it is only with a water-based paint immediately after baking. Thin layers paint is best recommended. Also, ensure that you seal your paint with several layers of Sculpey glaze.

Question: What does a pasta machine have to do with clay?

Answer: Pasta machines are used majorly for rolling, blending, and conditioning clay. You can easily condition stiff clay, especially when the hands are tired. Also, it aids the rolling out layers of uniform thickness in case of multiple similar products. They are very essential for making the beautiful Skinner blends.

Question: What do you need to begin?

Answer: The right fundamental knowledge, your hands, and the basic tools. you just need a clean, smooth, cool work surface. Marble glass, and ceramic tiles are the best work surfaces.

You just need a surface that is very smooth and not sticky to minimize disruption to the clay before baking, so that it can be well-conditioned and mixed. Other surface materials like wax paper, cardstock, index cards, and parchment paper can also be used for this purpose.

Question: How can polymer clay be stored?

Answer: Polymer clay should be stored in the original package, and away from harsh temperatures like heat or direct sunlight. Be careful where you keep it, do not leave the clay on open ground, or in your vehicle. It may bake itself if left in the open. Once the packaging has been opened, it is best to wrap it in wax paper and storing it in an airtight container. Avoid storing it in Tupperware or any food storage containers that you plan to use in storing food in the future. Ensure to store the clay in a very dry and cool place away from light. A perfect place is a refrigerator or freezer.

Question: What is the best polymer clay for kids?

Answer: The best brands of polymer clay there are is the Sculpey clay, and all the extensive brands under Sculpey are unique in themselves. Sculpey Bakeshop and Original Sculpey are soft and easy to use, which makes them a great choice for school projects and making simple children's projects. Bakeshop light is squishy and very light to use, it is perfect for making water toys because it floats after baking.

Beginners: They can use Sculpey III as it is easily manipulatable, and helps beginners to build their skills. It is an excellent choice for making simple household projects like simple jewelry making and more.

Professionals: They need to work with clay that allows for inserting details and precise color mixing. Premo Sculpey appears as the brilliant type of clay to use in that regard as it holds fine details and could be mixed evenly with any color.

Another or alternative to Premo is the Sculpey Souffle which is most ideal for very large projects and is simply lightweight.

Doll artists, sculptors, model makers, movie studios: They need something they can make to appear real, even though it is only imaginative. Something that will showcase their talent in realtime. Clays that you can try in this regard is the Super Sculpey.

Question: Is the over thermometer necessary?

Answer: Most certainly. You can't always trust that you will be guided by your senses to know when the accurate degrees required is set. Although some oven comes with a thermometer, if yours doesn't, you will have to purchase an external one.

Question: Can you bake polymer clay in a microwave?

Answer: No! it is unacceptable. Microwave cooks quickly at a very high temperature that you cannot really control in degrees. This harsh temperature is not good in any way for your clay, as it can cause it to break down, emit nauseating fumes, and burn. When something burns, even though it is nontoxic, it could produce smoke that irritates the lungs and eyes. Also, the heat in the microwave is uneven, and it will cause one part to harden while the other side remains soft or slightly unaffected.

It is best to cure your clay patiently and accurately in an oven if you really want your piece to come out strong.

Question: Can you air-dry polymer?

Answer: Yes, if you use air porcelain clay and other supply that could allow you to do that. But without them, you cannot air-dry polymer clay on its own. If you fail to introduce it to direct sunlight or steady heat from an oven, it will stay in its form. Actually, it could be like that for days.

Question: How long can polymer clay last?

Answer: If you store this clay properly, at the right temperature, it can last you years before it will become irrelevant or damaged. This is why many artists love this craft material. It is all about the right temperature.

Question: How do you soften polymer clay?

Answer: If your polymer clay has become hardened due to wrong exposure to harsh temperatures, you don't have to discard it. Try softening it with the Sculpey Liquid Clay Softener so that it is softer and has a more flexible texture. For four ounces of clay, you will need to add about eight to four drops of the softener. After adding it, attempt kneading the clay, don't knead too hard, start off slowly and knead the liquid in. It will go ahead and do its work. As the clay absorbs the liquid, it becomes softer.

144

Question: Do you paint polymer clay before or after baking?

Answer: The normal thing is to apply paint to already baked polymer clay, however, you can still apply it before baking. Depending on the effect you are going for. The best effect is gotten after the pieces are baked and hardened, then your color can easily reflect and shine brightly.

Also, it could be very challenging trying to paint a molded soft and slightly wet creation. Hence, you should use water-based acrylic paint after baking, it gives a perfect outlook. However, you can use any paint if you intend to apply a glaze. It will help retain the colors well.

Question: Why do artists use glaze?

Answer: A glaze is used to retain color and a small piece of clay.

You can use it to seal the piece with Sculpey Glaze, which will help preserve the colors.

It also helps you create the perfect finish that you want. The glossy glaze will add shine to your creation, and add an extra protective layer to increase its durability.

There are different types of glaze for different finishing effects.

Satin glaze helps to provide a smooth matte finish, and aids to add decorative details like metal leaf and glitter. You can use compatible floor waxes, water-based acrylics, or water-based fabric paints as sealers.

Before glazing, ensure that your model is buffed and sanded, after which you test the glaze by applying a little of the glaze to a very hidden portion of the piece. Then leave the material to completely interact well.

If the glaze is too thick, pour a few drops of water into the container and gently stir, place the cap back on the bottle and let it sit for an hour before use.

A glaze is a perfect finish to give your piece a complete and perfect look.

Question: How toxic is polymer clay?

Answer: This clay is not toxic, this is why you can bake it in your home oven freely. Although, it is advised that you still clean the surface of your kitchen tools used during curing, as it isn't also ingestible. You can't just ingest the clay into your stomach.

Also, if you use it directly on a food utensil, it is more difficult to clean totally with dish soap, as it is very porous.

Question: How do you make polymer clay firm up?

Answer: To change the consistency from soft to firmer clay, follow the simple steps.

- Protect the surface of your work
- Roll the clay into little sheets about a quarter of an inch thick
- Sandwich the sheets between the sheets of clean, white paper
- Place a book as a weight on top of the sheets of paper.

After about an hour, the paper surfaces will begin to look oily. The plasticizers coming out of the clay is what made it too soft.

You can change the paper a few times, and repeat the process until the clay reaches the desired softness.

Question: What is the best type of polymer clay for jewelry and earrings?

Answer: This confusion is not out of place, with all the numerous type of clay available in the market, you will be wondering what could probably be the best one that you could go for. As a beginner, the best brand you should go for is something like Sculpey Souffle or Sculpey Premo. It is easier to condition and blend. Especially the Premo brand, it provides medium firmness that works perfectly well on jewelry. Also, it is mostly available in online and offline stores.

For professional work, check out Fimo professional. It is firmer and has more artistic quality. To learn more about these types of polymer clay, you should check out chapter five.

Question: Why does clay fail to stay together after it has been baked?

Answer: It may be under baked. The strength of your finished pieces depends on how well you baked them. Under-baked clay is brittle and more likely to fall apart, unlike the well-baked clay.

Question: Can I bake polymer clay more than once?

Answer: Definitely Yes! You can bake polymer clay as many times as you want till you get your desired result. It is not out of place to return your clay to the oven if you feel it is not well baked. You could also bake parts of the clay and assemble them all later.

Question: How can I tell if a polymer is done baking?

Answer: Leave your clay in the oven for the stipulated time required for the project you are making. For every inch of thickness, ensure to leave your polymer clay for an average of 15 minutes baking. You can bring it out afterward. To evaluate the thickness, press the tip of your finger to the bottom of your piece, you will be able to feel the thickness of the clay. However, take note that as the clay cools off, it gets thicker.

Question: Can polymer clay be boiled?

Answer: Actually, boiling polymer clay could cure it and make it thick, but it won't give you the degree of thickness that you desire. Boiling water heats around 100 degrees, and your clay requires about 120-degree temperature to be properly cured and very thick.

Question: What is the best type of glue to use?

Answer: There is no perfect glue for all uses. As plastic, a polymer is flexible and can be used with various types of glue to keep it sturdy to different surfaces. A glue that looks fantastic on one material might not be on another. It is very easy to make mistakes. Always prepare the surface.

2-part epoxy is a great glue for work with polymer clay. It can brittle off with time and pop off. to bond metal to clay, you need to bake the metal with the clay. Glue can't hold it together

To bond polymer to wood, paper, fabric, use strong PVA glue.

Question: How do you make hard polymer clay soft?

Answer: A tip has been given already, but this is a faster way of softening your polymer clay.

Chop into tiny pieces and mash with a rolling pin until it is very flat. Use your hand to roll the clay into a circular ball. Massage it, and draw it into a snake shape. Roll the clay and grind it with a pasta machine.

Question: What else can I use with my clay?

Answer: Polymer clay works very well with other art materials and many of the products you already have for other crafts can be used with polymer clay. Experiment with mica powders, chalk powders, foils, acrylic paints, alcohol inks, Copic or Spectrum Noir markers, and acrylic inks. Rubber stamps, shape cutters, paper punches (on paper-thin sheets of baked clay), glitter, colored pencils, silicone molds, and epoxy resin are all commonly used with polymer clay and give you endless ways to create interesting results.

Conclusion

As the pages of this book have explained, your hands are the most basic tool you need to bring your innovations to reality, plus an enthusiastic, and highly imaginative mind. Polymer craft is very wide and interestingly so. It is an educative hands-on activity you can teach to kids in school or at home. They could even act as support aides or art assistants as you work. Hence, feel free to include them while working. So, if little kids can work through this clay, why can't you?

There is no point stocking up your storehouse with all the types of polymer tools before you set to working. This is common mistake beginner artists make that get them confused in the long run. There is no need for you to have all the tools before you begin. Waiting till you gather all the tools as a beginner could kill the enthusiasm and passion to learn in you. You could also get confused by the time you finally get them all. Stop buying products and stacking up tools and get your hands busy already.

Also, the basic project ideas you can start as a beginner have been discussed extensively you get you started.

They are simply basic and simple for anyone to try. Each project helps to build you a strong foundation in polymer craft and then you can go on to search for other ideas of polymer craft from Pinterest, and YouTube.

The journey to perfection or mastery in any craft can be very rough, but don't let your failures or mistakes limit you. In fact, expect them. Yes, you are bound to make mistakes, but don't let them discourage you from your journey to professionalism in polymer craft. Remember every artist was once an amateur.

If anyone can, you can do much more.

Now, go on and set that unique imagination on the oven already.

Printed in Great Britain
by Amazon